small business
accounting

Andy Lymer

For UK order enquiries: please contact Bookpoint Ltd,
130 Milton Park, Abingdon, Oxon OX14 4SB.
Telephone: +44 (0) 1235 827720. *Fax*: +44 (0) 1235 400454.
Lines are open 09.00–17.00, Monday to Saturday, with a
24-hour message answering service. Details about our titles
and how to order are available at www.hoddereducation.com

British Library Cataloguing in Publication Data: a catalogue record for this title
is available from the British Library.

First published in UK 2011 by Hodder Education, part of Hachette UK,
338 Euston Road, London NW1 3BH.

Typeset by MPS Limited, a Macmillan Company.

Printed in Great Britain for Hodder Education, an Hachette UK Company,
338 Euston Road, London NW1 3BH, by CPI Cox & Wyman, Reading,
Berkshire RG1 8EX.

The publisher has used its best endeavours to ensure that the URLs for
external websites referred to in this book are correct and active at the time of
going to press. However, the publisher and the author have no responsibility
for the websites and can make no guarantee that a site will remain live or
that the content will remain relevant, decent or appropriate.

Hachette UK's policy is to use papers that are natural, renewable and
recyclable products and made from wood grown in sustainable forests.
The logging and manufacturing processes are expected to conform to the
environmental regulations of the country of origin.

Impression number   10 9 8 7 6 5 4 3 2 1
Year   2015 2014 2013 2012 2011

Contents

Introduction

Who this book is aimed at

Many qualified accountants will recommend a similar system to the one discussed in this book when advising smaller business clients. The system is based around business bank statements, from which the figures are then analysed into various categories of income and expenditure. The method is what is referred to as single entry, with each business transaction being entered in the records only once.

The system requires nothing more than pencil and paper, although it does lend itself to being set up using a computerized spreadsheet program, eliminating much of the manual work involved in using a calculator to add up columns of figures.

As well as providing a tried and tested method to handle real business book-keeping, this book also demonstrates, using worked examples, how to keep business financial paperwork. It even provides guidance for completing your annual tax return.

Case studies

It is much easier to understand any system when you can see it in use, so three different case studies are used in this book.

Hardip Singh – builder

Hardip Singh is a builder. He has no permanent staff, but employs casual labourers from time to time.

Mr Singh's office is a table at his home, where he writes up his business records, and where his van and tools are kept overnight. He works on invoice, giving his customers a bill which they pay later. Sometimes he is paid immediately, either in cash or by cheque. He has a trade account with a local builders' merchant, but he also goes to DIY stores where he pays for materials by cheque or by credit card.

Grace Morris – shopkeeper

Grace Morris runs a village shop. The shop is rented, and she and her husband live in the flat upstairs. Mrs Morris's customers pay her as they purchase goods, in cash or by cheque. The exception is newspaper deliveries, for which people come into the shop and settle their bills once every two weeks or so.

Purchases are made partly from a large Cash and Carry store, and partly from wholesalers who invoice her.

Ben Martin – taxi driver

Ben Martin is a taxi driver. He works partly by picking up fares who hail him on the street, and partly by bookings made through another company, Cab-U-Like, which provides him with a two-way radio. He is almost always paid in cash by the customers he picks up from the street. However, when he takes a Cab-U-Like client he is not paid directly, but receives a cheque from Cab-U-Like in the first week of each month for the fares he carried during the previous month. Mr Martin's major running expenses are usually paid by credit card or by cheque, and he pays in cash for minor expenses.

Why this book is different and how to use it

If you have looked at other books on accountancy and book-keeping before buying this one, you will know that they are generally full of accounting jargon. They refer to ledgers and journals and 'double-entry' accounting, and you sometimes feel you need a dictionary by your side to read them. Do you really need to know all of this to handle the finances of a small business? No, of course you don't. Most of these books are not aimed primarily at owners of small businesses, they are written for students taking courses in book-keeping and accounts or set out a version of book-keeping better suited to much larger businesses. However, for many smaller businesses there is often no need to run a double-entry system if you don't want to.

The system described in this book enters accounting transactions using a single entry, and the series of case studies will guide you and also show you how to cope with some quite complex transactions.

At the end of your business year, you have a choice. If you choose to pay for an accountant to deal with your tax affairs, you can present him or her with a complete set of records, fully totalled and cross-referenced.

Alternatively you can deal with your own tax affairs. The records produced under the system here are designed so that they will produce the figures you will need to enter on your tax return, which has to be sent each year to HM Revenue & Customs.

1

your bank account

In this chapter the central role of the bank account as a tool for fully and accurately accounting for your business is explored. You are encouraged to keep a separate bank account for your business (not just your private account), to help make your accounting significantly easier in practice. Using internet banking is common these days, so we conclude the chapter with a brief discussion of how banking this way will help your business in practice.

Why you need a business bank account

For a small part-time business where customers pay in cash, a separate bank account for the business might not be needed. However, many successful businesses use a second (non-personal) bank account to undertake their business transactions. Once the number of business transactions rises above about a dozen or so each month (both purchases and sales combined) a more formal system for the recording and analysis of transactions is needed. By using a bank account solely for the business, separate from the owner's personal bank account, it is much easier to check the accounting records against the business bank statement, since all transactions must appear both in the records and on the bank statement.

Another good reason for using a separate business bank account is that it provides a degree of independent evidence for HM Revenue & Customs. Tax inspectors are wary of businesses conducted wholly or mainly in cash.

There are two other reasons why you might need a designated business account. The first is if you trade under a name other than your own. Banks normally accept cheques made payable only to the named account holder for a personal account. The second reason is if your business needs an overdraft facility. Banks will invariably ask why borrowing facilities are required, and are unlikely to grant business overdraft facilities for a personal account.

Case studies

So, how do the businesses in the case studies organize their banking needs?

Grace Morris would not be able to pay a cheque made out to 'Village Stores' into her personal account. In any case she needs to be able to pay in quite a lot of cash. She has therefore chosen a former building society that offers free business banking, as long as the account remains in credit, including facilities for paying in cash locally. The account is in the name of 'Grace Morris t/a Village Stores'.

The abbreviation 't/a' means 'trading as', allowing her to pay in cheques that are made out to either 'G Morris' or to 'Village Stores'. This can save her a lot of hassle in getting cheques redone when people use the wrong name.

Hardip Singh trades under his own name, but needs an overdraft facility to allow him to pay suppliers for materials and labour that he can bill to the customer only once a building job is completed. He therefore needs a business account with a bank. He did not use the bank that holds his personal account, however, but instead asked other local builders. He found that several of them used a bank that had a branch in the local high street and where the staff understood the financial issues that face all builders.

Like Mrs Morris, Ben Martin cannot use a personal account because of the amount of cash that he banks each day. However, if he worked mainly for Cab-U-Like clients, so that most of his bankings came in the form of a single monthly cheque from Cab-U-Like, he might have been able to utilize a private account. However, given the cash factor, Mr Martin also uses a business bank account at a high street bank.

Internet banking

Internet banking, available for businesses as well as for individuals, lets you view your account balances, transfer funds between accounts, and pay bills and wages online. Online bank statements are also available.

Internet banking can provide small businesses with a number of advantages in terms of ready access to their bank accounts, rapid processing of bills, ability to set up payments in advance, change standing orders and direct debits, and so on. Many businesses find using internet banking improves their efficiency in handling their accounts.

2

a simple cashbook

At the heart of the simple accounting system proposed in this book is what is called 'the cashbook'. As its name might suggest, this is an accounting record you keep of everything you do with the cash belonging to your business – both spending it and receiving it. This chapter introduces you to the cashbook, shows you the basics of how to create one and outlines how to keep details of your various business transactions using it.

Confusingly, a cashbook does not normally show what has happened to the cash in your business, it shows what has happened to money you have paid into or taken out of the bank. If you want to think of it as a bank book that is fine, but it is referred to here as a cashbook because that is what it will be called by an accountant or the tax inspector.

In essence, a cashbook is not much more than a detailed bank statement. It brings together in a single business record all the information normally put on cheque-book stubs and paying-in slips to identify exactly what payments have been made and what receipts have been received.

Hardip Singh's simple cashbook

In the Introduction you met Hardip Singh, a builder. Figure 2.1 shows his bank statement for the month of June.

The following further information is as recorded by him on his cheque-book stubs, plus it shows the regular standing orders paid out from the account.

* Cheque 1000234 was to High St Garage for diesel for his van.
* Cheque 1000235 was to the Anytown Courier for an advertisement.
* Cheque 1000236 was to Browns for stationery.
* Cheque 1000237 was to Smarts Builders' Merchants for supplies, of which £30 was for use in his own home.
* Cheque 1000238 was to Jones Plumbing for supplies.
* Cheque 1000239 was to Post Office Limited for car tax (Road Fund Licence) on the van.
* Cheque 1000241 was to Print Presto for business cards and letterheads.
* The standing order payment to County Leasing is the monthly instalment on the lease contract for the van, and the payment to Magnificent Mutual is for his personal pension.

* The direct debit payment to NICO is to the National Insurance Contributions Office for his Class 2 National Insurance Contributions (NICs). Your total might not be the same as Hardip's is here, as this varies from year to year.
* The payment to H. Singh is the money he takes out of the business each month for his living needs and private use; it is known as monthly 'Drawings' and is paid into his personal bank account.

		Debit	Credit	Balance
1 June	Balance b/f			2150.25
3 June	s/o County Leasing	345.22		1805.03
8 June	Ch 1000234	28.34		1776.69
10 June	Dep 6000132		396.75	2173.44
10 June	Ch 1000236	25.68		2147.76
12 June	s/o H. Singh	500.00		1647.76
14 June	Charges	42.30		1605.46
18 June	Ch 1000235	43.69		1561.77
18 June	Ch 1000237	692.59		869.18
20 June	Dep 6000133		2750.00	3619.18
21 June	DD NICO	28.40		3590.78
23 June	Ch 1000238	254.00		3336.78
23 June	Ch 1000239	150.00		3186.78
28 June	Ch 1000241	82.38		3104.40
30 June	DD Mag. Mutual	100.00		3004.40
30 June	Balance b/f			3004.40

Figure 2.1 *Hardip Singh's bank statement.*

Mr Singh issues an invoice from a pre-numbered duplicate book for each building job done (see Figure 2.1).

* Deposit number 6000132 was a cheque from Mr Henderson paying invoice 121.
* Deposit 6000133 was a cheque for £2,000 from Mr Peters paying invoice number 118, a cheque for £600 from Dr Bull paying invoice number 119 and £150 in cash from Mr Blunt paying invoice number 123.

Mr Singh writes his cashbook up at the end of each month when he receives his bank statement. He uses a two-column cashbook, so that he can enter subtotals, and he writes receipts on the left-hand page and payments on the right. Figure 2.2 shows his Payments page for June.

PAYMENTS

3 June	s/o County Leasing	(Motor)		345.22
8 June	234 High St Garage	(Motor)		28.34
10 June	236 V G Browns	(Administration)		25.68
12 June	s/o H. Singh	(Drawings)		500.00
14 June	Charges	(Finance charges)		42.30
18 June	235 Anytown Courier	(Advertising)		43.69
18 June	237 Smarts	(Cost of Sales)	662.59	
	237 Smarts	(Drawings)	30.00	692.59
21 June	DD NICO	(Drawings)		28.40
23 June	238 Jones Plumbing	(Cost of Sales)		254.00
23 June	239 Post Office Limited	(Motor)		150.00
28 June	241 Print Presto	(Administration)		82.38
30 June	DD Magnificent Mutual	(Drawings)		100.00
30 June	Total			2292.60

Figure 2.2 *Hardip Singh's payments.*

Notes

1 Each entry shows the cheque number, the payee to whom the payment was made, and the type of expense (shown in brackets). Some of these will be obvious; for example Road Fund Licence and petrol are classed as 'Motor'. Some will not be so obvious, such as 'Cost of sales'. The reason for using these specific headings rather than choosing ones that may be more appropriate to Mr Singh's business is that they are the ones he will need to use when filling in his tax return. By using these categories right from the start, filling in the tax return will be made much easier. The types of payment to be included in each category are set out in the next chapter.

2 Money taken out of the business for the owner's personal use is 'Drawings' and this will include payments to the owner's pension plan, and any tax and national insurance payments. The latter are not expenses of the business, they are the owner's private liability.

3 As long as cheques run in a numerical sequence from one cheque book to the next, only the last three digits may be needed.

4 The total payment to Smarts included £30 of materials that were for Mr Singh's private usage, and so must be recorded as drawings. Be careful always to do this when you take materials for your own use or you'll get into trouble with your tax reporting where you must get this right. Two cashbook entries are thus made for the same cheque, with amounts in the first column that add up to the subtotal amount of the cheque, which is entered in the second column.

5 All the payments shown are inclusive of any VAT charged.

Mr Singh's Receipts page (i.e. the left-hand page to his cashbook) for June is shown in Figure 2.3.

Notes

1 Mr Singh writes up his records only when he receives his monthly bank statement, and so the balance brought forward of £2150.25 will be the same in his cashbook and on the bank statement. It is included on the 'Receipts' side of the page because he is in credit at the bank. If he had been overdrawn the balance would be brought forward on the 'Payments' side.

2 In this example the bankings for each separate invoice have been listed and totalled.

3 The fact that some of the receipts were in cash and some were cheques does not matter, since they were all paid in to the bank. When cash received is not all paid in to the bank, a way has to be found of entering it in the cashbook, as will be explained in the next example.

RECEIPTS			
1 June	Brought forward		2150.25
10 June	132 Henderson (Invoice 121)		396.75
20 June	133 Peters (Invoice 118)	2000.00	
	133 Bull (Invoice 119)	600.00	
	133 Blunt (Invoice 123)	150.00	2750.00
30 June	TOTAL		5297.00
	Less payments		2292.60
			3004.40

Figure 2.3 *Hardip Singh's receipts.*

When to update the cashbook

There are two possible ways of updating the cashbook. It can either be prepared from the bank statement after that has been received, as in Hardip Singh's case, or it can be written up as you go along, and then compared (called reconciled) to the bank statement when that comes in. Different approaches will suit different businesses.

One advantage of updating the cashbook once the bank statement is received is that it is easier to compare the two. The final balance shown on the cashbook should always agree with the final balance on the statement, thus making it easier to identify mistakes. It may also take less time to sit down for a couple of hours each month with all the necessary records to hand and update the cashbook in one go, rather than spending time doing it each day or even once per week.

Conversely, the advantage of keeping the cashbook up to date as you go along is that you always know what your true balance at the bank is, if all cheques you have written had been cashed and if all bankings made had been credited to the account.

Cashbook analysis

The cashbook provides the most fundamental financial record for each business. However, it won't immediately show the owner how the receipts and payments under various different headings combine overall. By looking back at Mr Singh's cashbook, it is quite easy to see how a statement showing his receipts and payments could be prepared from it. Total receipts in the month were £3,146.75, being the £5,297.00 total shown on the Receipts page of the cashbook less the £2,150.25 that he had started with at the beginning of the month. For payments, the various entries on the Payments page can be totalled using their various expense categories, as shown in Figure 2.4.

Motor	(345.22 + 28.34 + 150)	£523.56
Administration	(25.68 + 82.38)	£108.06
Drawings	(500 + 30 + 28.40 + 100)	£658.40
Finance charges		£42.30
Advertising		£43.69
Cost of sales	(662.59 + 254)	£916.59

Figure 2.4 *Hardip Singh – expenses.*

In order to simplify the process of calculating totals for each category and for each month, the simple two-column cashbook can be expanded so that each amount is recorded first of all in a total column, and then secondly in a separate column set up for each individual expense or receipt category. This format is commonly known as an 'analysed cashbook', and is at the heart of the accounting system set out in this book.

Layout

Figure 2.5 shows how the payments side of Mr Singh's original two-column cashbook, as seen in the last chapter, would look when set out in full analysed cashbook format. If this looks somewhat daunting simply compare it with Figure 2.2 and you will find that the differences are really quite straightforward.

The first two columns of the analysed cashbook are almost exactly the same as the first two columns of the simple cashbook, showing the date and the details of the payments from the bank statement. The third column of the analysed cashbook is exactly the same as the last column of the two-column cashbook, it shows amounts paid out of the bank account, just as before.

However, you will now notice additional columns on the right of the 'Total' column, each one headed up with one of the categories of expenditure, the categories previously recorded as part of the details of the payment in the original simple cashbook. There were six categories used, so six additional columns are needed to do the analysis.

Looking at the first entry, £345.22 paid to County Leasing for van rental, this was categorized in the two-column cashbook as 'Motor'. In the analysed cashbook, as well as the sum of £345.22 being entered in the 'Total' column, it is also entered under the 'Motor' column.

Date	Details	Total	Motor	Admin.	Drawings	Finance	Advertising	Cost of sales
3 Jun	s/o County Leasing	345.22	345.22					
8 Jun	234 High St Garage	28.34	28.34					
10 Jun	236 V G Browns	25.68		25.68				
12 Jun	s/o H Singh	500.00			500.00			
14 Jun	Charges	42.30				42.30		
18 Jun	235 Anytown Courier	43.69					43.69	
18 Jun	237 Smarts	692.59			30.00			662.59
21 Jun	DD NICO	28.40			28.40			
23 Jun	238 Jones Plumb.	254.00						254.00
23 Jun	239 Post Office Ltd.	150.00	150.00					
28 Jun	241 Print Presto	82.38		82.38				
30 Jun	DD Magnificent Mutual	100.00			100.00			
30 Jun	TOTALS	2,292.60	523.56	108.06	658.40	42.30	43.69	916.59

Figure 2.5 *Hardip Singh – analysed payments for June.*

The next payment is cheque number 234 to High St Garage. This is also a motoring expense, so £28.34 is entered in the 'Total' column and under the 'Motor' column.

All the other entries are made in the same way, but note particularly the entry for 18 June, cheque number 237 to Smarts. The total of £692.59 was made up of £30 for goods used privately, categorized as 'Drawings', with the balance of £662.59 reflecting the cost of materials used on a building job, categorized as 'Cost of sales'. In the simple cashbook these were entered as separate figures and then totalled up. However, in the analysed cashbook, the full £692.59 is entered in the 'Total' column, then £30.00 entered under 'Drawings' and £662.59 entered under 'Cost of sales'. Note carefully that exactly the same information is recorded, but the way that the information is set out under each method is different.

Figure 2.5 illustrates an important point about analysed cashbooks. For each entry, the total of the amounts entered in the detailed analysis columns will be exactly the same as the amount entered in the total column. Provided a business is not VAT-registered (we will talk about VAT in Chapter 9), most entries will have only one amount in an analysis column, which matches the amount in the 'Total' column. If, as for the Smarts entry, the expenditure relates to more than one category, the total under all of the separate columns will always add up to the amount shown by the 'Total' column.

Looking at the totals, it now becomes clear that it is quite easy for Mr Singh to total up the expenditure under each category heading, and that is the main reason for using separate analysis columns. For example, when using the two-column cashbook there were four different entries categorized as 'Drawings' scattered over the page. Making sure that he didn't miss any in calculating the total for drawings in Figure 2.4 could have been difficult, especially if there had been 50 entries rather than 12. If you compare the payments summary in Figure 2.2 with the totals for each column in Figure 2.5, you will see that they match.

Another important point to note is that when added together the totals of the analysis columns will be the same as the total of the 'Total' column. In other words, looking at Figure 2.5, £(523.56 + 108.06 + 658.40 + 42.30 + 43.69 + 916.59) gives a total of £2,292.60. If this cross-checking process does not work then an error must have occurred somewhere.

Expense categories

The column headings for analysis by this system are based around the categories required by HM Revenue & Customs in the UK self-assessment tax return. These are listed below, together with details of what should be included under each heading. Some will be self-evident, others may be slightly surprising, and you may want to return to this chapter on occasion in order to decide which standard category covers a particular expense item.

The following broad descriptions of the category headings are a starting point:

The 'Cost of sales' category should be used for costs of supplies and raw materials that are used directly in making a product or delivering a service. Cab drivers and transport businesses would normally include their fuel costs here in view of the nature of their businesses, but for most others the costs of fuel would be what is known as an 'overhead' and allocated into the category of motor expenses.

The 'Subcontractors' heading should be used only by businesses in the construction industry for payments to subcontractors. Payments to subcontract staff in other businesses, such as payments to a locum vet or GP, should be allocated to employee costs.

'Other direct costs': there are relatively few expenses that fall into this category. Include hire costs of machinery here (other than motor vehicles) and rechargeable expenses. These are any expenses that you incur but which you subsequently recover from customers. If you are not sure whether an expense belongs here or in another category, it is probably the latter.

'Employee costs' consist of not just employee salaries, but (as noted above) payments to subcontractors other than construction industry subcontractors, and payments to recruitment agencies for any temporary or contract staff. Do not include what you may refer to as your own 'wages'; these are in fact drawings from the business.

'Premises' costs include rent, heat, light and insurance. For the typical small business operating from the owner's home, an adjustment at the end of the year for what is known as 'use of home as office' may be all that is needed. This is covered in Chapter 10.

'Repairs' covers both the maintenance of business premises and machinery repairs. Note that any 'improvements' cannot be claimed against tax, and so professional advice may be needed.

'General administrative expenses' is a catch-all heading for office expenses such as telephone, stationery, postage and business subscriptions. This is where a lot of expenses for most businesses will end up.

'Motor expenses' are relatively self-explanatory, but note that car repairs will normally go here, not under the repairs category.

'Travel and subsistence' costs include any travel other than motor expenses, plus the cost of any hotel accommodation while away on business trips. There are specific rules about claiming for meals and subsistence, and these will be worth checking if you stay away on business to ensure that you claim as much as is legitimately possible. Remember always that if you don't claim for a cost that you are entitled to claim for, it is unlikely that the tax inspector will suggest that you should be claiming it! Not least, he or she will probably be unaware that you have incurred it.

The 'Advertising' heading also includes cost of direct mail and promotional activity. Entertainment costs for customers and suppliers is never tax allowable, although entertainment of employees can be allowable up to a maximum amount per employee per year.

'Legal and professional fees' will include payments to lawyers, accountants and architects, for example. You cannot, however, claim fees which relate to the purchase of fixed assets such as machinery or property.

'Interest' costs should be self-explanatory.

'Other finance charges' relates to bank and other finance costs other than interest charges.

'Other business expenses' is another broad category, but as noted earlier many general expenses will fall under the general administrative costs heading.

'Drawings' will include all payments that are for private purposes rather than business costs. This includes the owner's tax and national insurance bill.

'Purchase of equipment' is dealt with in Chapter 5, but this is the heading to use to record so-called 'capital' payments where long-term assets (ones you typically will keep for more than 12 months) are being acquired, such as furniture, vehicles and equipment.

3

payments

In this chapter we look in more detail at how to deal with the things you have to pay for to run your business – your payments or 'expenses'. This includes practical suggestions on how to keep track of all the paperwork that quickly accumulates as you run a business, and also how to correctly enter all the necessary details into your cashbook. We also suggest how to keep your cheque book up to date so you can easily trace how this has been used in making payments.

Filing invoices

There are three basic rules for filing invoices:

1 The invoices are filed in the order that you pay them, not when they are received.
2 Each invoice has written on it the date of payment and the number of the cheque sent in payment.
3 Invoices are kept on top of a dividing card while they remain unpaid, and filed underneath it when they have been paid.

Example

It is 31 March. Grace Morris has just been to the local Cash and Carry store and purchased stock costing £856. She paid by cheque, number 456. On the way back she put petrol into her estate car, paying £20 using cheque number 457.

The example below shows how Mrs Morris dealt with these transactions.

The invoices will be filed in the order in which they were paid from the cheque book. The first cheque written by Mrs Morris was number 456 for £856.00 to the Cash and Carry store. She duly wrote '456' on the invoice itself as a record, and circled it so that it could easily be seen, and added the words 'Paid 31/3'. She then filed the invoice immediately.

The next cheque she wrote was number 457, for £20 of petrol. She kept the till receipt as evidence of the petrol purchase, and later stapled it to a larger sheet of A4 paper, writing 'Petrol, £20' on the A4 sheet. She added '457' to indicate the cheque number, and 'Paid 31/3' on the A4 sheet, and filed it on top of the Cash and Carry invoice, below the divider card.

Managing your creditors

The people to whom money is owed for goods or services supplied on credit terms are known as creditors, and managing payments to creditors is an important part of running a business. Payment dates have a direct impact upon the bank balance.

It will improve your credit rating with suppliers if you pay them on time, but unless they offer an 'early settlement discount', that is offer you a discount if you pay them promptly, there is not much point in paying them in advance of their normal terms. If you are offered 28 days to pay, take that length of time – do not pay as soon as you get the invoice. It is better for you to keep your bank balance as healthy as possible by having the money in your account. If you think about it carefully, you will realize that until you pay them, your creditors are in fact supplying interest-free funds to your business!

Supplier statements

Some suppliers will send you monthly statements, showing a breakdown of what you owe them. These can be a useful check for you too, but be careful not to file these as if they were invoices, or you may end up paying the same bill twice. Use statements to check that the invoices shown as unpaid on the statement are still filed as unpaid.

No invoices

Not every business payment will have an invoice, but each should have some sort of supporting documentation or notes on the lever-arch file. If it is a personal payment, which is clearly marked on the cheque-book stub as drawings, then this is not so important, but it is a legal requirement that you keep business records which are sufficient to justify your business expenses.

Example

Hardip Singh paid a neighbour £25 by cheque for the use of her garage to store some machinery for a few weeks. The neighbour did not provide any form of receipt. Mr Singh duly made a note on an A4 sheet of paper 'Paid to Mrs Owen for use of garage to store machinery, £25' and wrote on it the cheque number and the date of payment in the usual way. This was filed in the supplier lever-arch file in the same place as an invoice would have been filed. It would have been better to have obtained a receipt for the payment from Mrs Owen, but at least a supporting record was created with a clear explanation of why this was a bona fide business payment.

In this chapter there have been several references to writing cheques. Completing these, and completing cheque-book stubs correctly may seem obvious but is actually surprisingly important to get right.

The aim of the system for recording payments is to ensure that all essential details are recorded in at least two places. In that way, if records are mislaid, such as a set of cheque-book stubs, or a file of invoices, or even your cashbook for a year, it becomes possible to reconstruct what has been lost from the other information held.

The importance of payment details

First and foremost a cheque-book stub must record the purpose of a payment. The main aim of the book-keeping system is to identify items of business income and expenses and record them under the appropriate category headings for submission to HM Revenue & Customs in due course. For example, if an electricity bill is paid by cheque, the most important thing to write on the cheque stub is 'Electricity' (or something similar) as an accurate and adequate description of what the payment was for in case you needed to refer to it at a later date.

The next most important piece of information is to state to whom the cheque was paid. In the case of an electricity bill that mostly likely would be the name of your energy supplier. If a cheque stub doesn't state clearly to whom a payment has been made then it might later be misinterpreted as being for something else.

The cheque stub should also note the date that the invoice being paid was raised. This lets the business owner check in either the cheque book or the supplier invoice file whether a particular purchase invoice has been paid.

Also record the date that a cheque is being paid, since the only other place that this is recorded will be in the supplier invoice file.

Finally, note on the stub the amount that the cheque was made out for. However, if you forget you will be able to find the amount on the invoice and confirm that you made the cheque out for that amount when your bank statement arrives. In practice, most people remember to write in the amount on the stub, but it is in fact the purpose, both relevant dates, and the payee name which they may omit. It is far more difficult, and time-consuming, to get these details right later although it takes just a matter of seconds to complete them on the stub at the time that the cheque is written.

Missing details

It is quite possible that having read through the recommendations for record-keeping above, these seem to be a detailed explanation of the rather obvious. In practice, when accountants are preparing business accounts from the books and accounts of small businesses they often find that cheque-book stub details are missing or incomplete. It is also worth remembering that a scribbled note that makes perfect sense to you when you write it may not mean anything when you are asked to explain it by your tax inspector or VAT officer a year or two later. The habit of filling in your cheque stubs correctly will serve you well! You may want to note down the following five points inside the cover of your cheque-book, so that you remember to complete all relevant details.

1 Purpose
2 Payee
3 Invoice date
4 Date written
5 Amount

Finally in this chapter we look at using analysis columns to record payments. The example given in the previous chapter showed the basic principle of the analysis into different columns; this chapter shows the method being used for a more complex example.

Buying a cashbook

Suitable analysis cashbooks are sold in stationery shops. They are approximately A3 size, the size of two standard sheets of A4 paper side by side. There is space left available at the top for the overall heading and space at the top of each column for the analysis headings. The left-most three columns are different from the others. The first will be used to record the date, the second is wider to allow for written details, such as the name of the person to whom a cheque was payable, and the third column is a narrow one, and sometimes referred to as the folio column. It would typically be used to record cheque numbers.

After that there are columns used for recording the analysed amounts. To give plenty of space, many people select a 32-column analysed cashbook, which means 32-columns in addition to the first three.

Heading up the cashbook

Inside the front cover of the book insert your name and contact details. Even if you intend to deal with your own affairs, it may be necessary at some point for the book to be sent to your accountant or for examination by HM Revenue & Customs, and clear labelling is an insurance policy against it being lost in a large office, as has been known to happen.

It is easiest to start the book at the beginning of a business year, if possible. At the top of the page, write in the name of the bank, the sort code and the account number. Apart from being an easy place to find these details when you want them, this will prevent problems in matching up the cashbook to the bank statements if the business changes banks. Also write in the month and year, and start a new page at the beginning of each month.

Head up the left-most column as 'Date'. The next (wide) column should be labelled 'Payments out', and the small column headed as 'Cheque number'.

The next column, the first monetary column, should be headed 'Total'. Leave the following column blank: you will use it later when checking off the payments to the bank statement, and to note any brought-forward bank overdraft figure. Head up the columns following with the categories listed in Chapter 2, missing out any that you will not need for your business. List them in the order that they are given in Chapter 2, which will also be the correct order for the same categories on your tax return. This may take up to the sixteenth column, depending on which headings are being used.

Leave the other columns blank; they will be used later for receipts headings, as will be explained in Chapter 7. If you are VAT-registered, you will also need a column for VAT, as will be explained in Chapter 9.

Writing up the cashbook

To start using the cashbook, enter first the latest balance shown on the bank statement, adjusting if necessary for any cheques written and deposits made before the cashbook start date but which, for timing reasons, are not reflected in the bank statement at that date. You need to make this adjustment only if you will be writing up the books from your records as you go along; if you are going to write them up when they appear on the bank statement then simply start with the opening balance on the statement.

The reason for entering the opening balance is to allow easy checking of your bank balance. Adding all the figures in a 'Payments in' (Receipts) Total column and in the 'Payments out' Total column, and then subtracting the second total from the first will give the latest bank balance, positive if the balance is in credit and negative if it is overdrawn.

Bank account no 123 456 23   Sort code 22-22-22   June 201X

Date	Payments out	Cheque no.	Total	Cost of sales	Employees	Admin.	Motor	Travel	Advertising	Legal/ Prof.	Finance	Drawings
1 Jun	Bal b/f		2,040.53	2,040.53								
3 Jun	s/o County Leasing		345.22				345.22					
8 Jun	High St Garage	234	28.34				28.34					
10 Jun	V G Browns		25.68			25.68						
12 Jun	s/o H Singh		500.00									500.00
14 Jun	Charges		42.30							42.30		
18 Jun	Anytown Courier	235	43.69						43.69			
18 Jun	Smarts	237	692.59	662.59								30.00
21 Jun	DD NICO		28.40									28.40
23 Jun	Jones Plumb.	238	254.00	254.00								
23 Jun	Post Office Limited	239	150.00				150.00					
28 Jun	Print Presto	241	82.38			82.38						
30 Jun	d/d Magnificent Mutual		100.00									100.00
30 Jun	TOTALS		4333.13	2,040.53	916.59	108.06	523.56		43.69	42.30	42.30	658.40

Figure 3.1 Hardip Singh's payments page – June.

If the bank balance brought forward at the start date is positive (i.e. you are in credit at the bank) this should be written in the first line of the Total column for payments in. If the balance is overdrawn it will go in the first line of the Total column for payments out. Simply enter the date, write 'Balance b/f' (brought forward) in the details, nothing under 'Cheque number', and the balance under 'Total'.

Figure 3.1 shows the payments side of Mr Singh's cashbook again, although the balance brought forward has now been changed. More columns have been included, in the order set out in Chapter 2. The last columns, not needed for the entries given, have not been shown in order to make the illustration clearer.

Note that a balance brought forward of £2,040.53 appears on the payments side. Mr Singh's business was overdrawn by this amount according to his bank statement on 1 June. He writes up his cashbook only when he receives the bank statement and therefore does not need to adjust the opening balance for any uncleared items. The Total column now includes the 'opening' overdraft figure, and so not only shows the amount that has been spent during the month, it reveals the amount by which the business would be overdrawn if all the payments out had been made but nothing paid into the account.

4

non-allowable expenses

Not all payments you make for your business will be allowed as deductions when computing your tax bill – even though you have spent the money buying things for your business. In this chapter we look in more detail at which payments can be deducted and which ones can't.

This chapter reviews the types of expenditure that may not be allowable as deductions in your tax calculation, but also highlights less obvious expenses that can be used to reduce your tax bill.

The 'wholly and exclusively' rule

The most important general rule is that an expense will be allowable against tax only if it is incurred 'wholly and exclusively' for business purposes. When this rule is applied strictly it can be harsh.

Sometimes in practice, however, tax inspectors may be willing to split a cost as part business and part private on an appropriate percentage basis, but be careful about discussing any private element to any expense, since strictly speaking that disbars it from being tax allowable. (Of course, you have to be truthful and own up to any private elements if there are any – the tax inspector will not be happy to find this out later.)

Revenue expenditure versus capital expenditure

A second key tax concept is that an allowable expense must be a 'revenue' expense, broadly a cost that is charged to the business profit and loss account, rather than a 'capital' item. Certain capital expenditure, mainly the purchase of plant, machinery and equipment, including vehicles, receives a separate tax relief via 'capital allowances'. Details of how to record the purchase of capital equipment are included in the next chapter, and the calculation of capital allowances is outlined.

These two tax concepts, 'wholly and exclusively' and 'revenue versus capital', are commonly encountered sources of tax disallowances. The areas listed below are a general guide; always seek further advice if you are unsure.

Loans

Interest charged on a loan taken out for business purposes is normally a tax-deductible revenue expense, whereas any repayment of the capital amount itself is not.

Leases and hire purchase

If business assets such as equipment are leased or rented, so that you never actually own them, the full rental expense is normally allowable against tax.

If the contract involves the purchase of the asset however, or gives the right to purchase the asset, such as applies under lease purchase arrangements, then the correct tax treatment is to treat the asset as if it had been owned from the outset. Payments made to the finance company under the contract are then a combination of loan repayments and interest charges.

Motor expenses

The area of tax allowances for vehicles is a particularly complex one and you may decide to consult a qualified accountant for advice on your specific situation. HM Revenue & Customs will permit a claim against tax for the proportion of total motor expenses that matches the proportion of business mileage to total mileage. Thus if total mileage is 10,000 per annum, and 8,000 miles of that total was for business travel, then 80% of total motor expenses could be claimed against tax. All expenses should be recorded and entered onto the tax return and then an entry made for the amount disallowed, one-fifth in this particular example. The disallowed amount should be written in the box for disallowable expenses to show the tax inspector clearly that the non-business proportion of motor expenses has not been deducted against tax.

Subscriptions

Membership fees for professional and trade bodies and Chambers of Commerce are normally allowable against tax. However, even if you find them useful for business purposes, HM Revenue & Customs will normally disallow costs such as sports and social club memberships.

Entertainment

Entertainment expenditure, except for staff entertainment, is not tax allowable at all. You may hear that it is allowable if you are entertaining foreign customers; this was once true but has long-since been abolished. The disallowance extends to 'business lunches', whether or not you really find lunch with your biggest customer or supplier more of an ordeal than a pleasure!

Entertaining of employees can be tax deductible up to a fixed amount each year; this does not have to be spent all in one go at Christmas despite the fact that the allowance is often referred to as the 'Christmas Party Allowance'.

Hotels and subsistence

Overnight stays away on business are tax allowable for accommodation and for the cost of meals. The rules can vary according to the nature of your business. Note that if you do not stay away overnight, you cannot normally claim the cost of meals, even for a business trip that takes all day and forces you to eat away from home.

Travel

Travel from your normal place of business to a customer is tax allowable, but note that travel from home to your place of business is not allowable. Disputes can arise with the tax inspector if a contract leads you to spend substantial periods at a client's own premises, and HM Revenue & Customs may seek to disallow the cost of travelling there from your home. Guidelines exist about the proportion of total time spent at a given client's premises which may trigger travel costs being disallowed. It would be wise if you are in this situation to take professional advice and avoid an unpleasant shock later.

Ensure also that you can demonstrate that your business is operated from home, and that you normally work from there, store equipment there, and that your accounting books and records are maintained there.

Allowable expenses

Here are a few more unusual expenses that may be tax allowable:

Newspapers and magazines may be allowable if they are used for business and research.

Special protective garments will generally be allowable as an expense.

If you use part of your home as an office then certain expenses of running the home may be tax allowable, but it may be simplest to estimate the expense by claiming a small fixed sum per week.

Grace Morris might claim against tax for (say) one-half of the rent, light, heat and other expenses of the whole property, since the shop premises are downstairs. She might actually argue for a higher percentage for certain costs on the grounds, for example, that the shop uses more light, heat and power than does the flat. Ben Martin would be unwise to try to claim more than a couple of pounds per week, since he spends most of his working time away from home. However, he writes up his books and records there, keeps his taxi in the garage overnight, and sometimes works on it at weekends, so a small claim would be in order. Hardip Singh uses his spare bedroom as an office, and his garage is used to store building materials, and so a claim against tax for some of his domestic running costs would be justified.

5

purchase of equipment

In Chapter 4 we looked at which regular expenses can be deducted from your tax bill each year, and which can not. In this chapter we look at how purchasing equipment and similar items is handled in your cashbook recording process compared to the smaller regular payments we have looked at so far. We also introduce you to what the taxman calls 'capital allowances', which detail what you can deduct for these purchases from your tax bill each year. This is important as you can't normally just deduct what you have spent on equipment as you spend it.

You will know from the last chapter that capital expenditure is not tax deductible when spent in the way that revenue expenses are. However, the purchase of equipment such as computers, machinery and vehicles does get tax relief, under the system of 'capital allowances' that applies in the UK. This allows you to deduct part of any capital expenditure for each year you own or use the asset.

This chapter looks at the process of recording the purchase of items of capital equipment and then calculating the capital allowances on them.

Recording transactions

Outright purchases of equipment are simple to record. The amount paid is shown in the 'Total' column, and then also included in the 'Purchase of equipment' column.

Equipment may also be acquired in instalments, through a hire purchase or lease purchase arrangement; or a loan may be taken out to finance the purchase. These types of transactions are more complicated to handle.

One way to deal with these, although unorthodox in accounting terms, is to record two opposing (called contra) entries: the first being the purchase of the asset for the full cash price; the other as capital introduced into the business. These entries record that you as the business owner have put the money into the business in order to buy the asset. The fact that you were able to do so by borrowing the money does not change things. As a result, the capital repayments each month or quarter can then be posted under 'Drawings'. The interest element goes to other finance charges, and will be an allowable expense for tax purposes.

Example

Grace Morris buys a new freezer for the shop for £3,000, and will pay for it in 12 instalments of £300 each. Because it is a short credit agreement, she decides to use the simple calculation method above to decide how much of each payment is capital and how much is interest.

£3,000 ÷ 12 = £250

Therefore £250 of each monthly £300 payment is capital, that is to say repayment of the original sum borrowed, and the balance of £50 is interest charged.

Figure 5.1 shows two entries in Mrs Morris's cashbook. The first is the entry for the initial purchase and the loan. There is no cheque number, because she has not had to pay out the £3,000 as she has arranged finance for it. The £3,000 expenditure is, therefore, a contra entry with a similar entry shown in receipts as capital introduced. The subject of capital introduced is dealt with in more detail in Chapter 8. The net effect is to leave the bank balance itself unchanged, as indeed it should be since no money has actually gone out of the business at this point, and the acquisition of the freezer at the purchase price of £3,000 is now reflected in the books.

The second entry is that needed for each of the 12 monthly payments of £300. Following the calculation above, £250 is posted into the drawings column and the remaining £50 is recorded as an interest payment.

Capital introduced is, in fact, simply the opposite of drawings; it is money put into the business rather than money taken out. Just as the initial loan was shown as capital introduced, the repayments are recorded as drawings. The rest of the figure shows in summary form all entries connected with the purchase of the freezer. The totals at the bottom of the analysis show the sum of £3,000 for purchase of equipment, which correctly records the cash price of the freezer, plus £600 of interest charges, which is the total interest suffered. Total payments are thus (£300 × 12) £3,600. Finally there are two total entries for £3,000, one under drawings and one under capital introduced. These entries are needed to record that Mrs Morris withdrew £3,000 from the business, having previously injected £3,000 into it. The two amounts offset each other, and therefore have no net effect on the accounts.

Under the system in this book any receipts from the sale of equipment are simply recorded as a negative expense, subtracted from the figures on the payments side of the book.

Date	Payments out	Total	Equipment	Drawings	Finance	Date	Payments in	Total	Capital int.
1 1X	Freezer (paid by loan)	3,000.00	3,000.00			1 1X	Contra for freezer loan	3,000.00	3,000.00
Mth 1	Repayment	300.00		250.00	50.00				
Mth 2	Repayment	300.00		250.00	50.00				
Mth 3	Repayment	300.00		250.00	50.00				
Mth 4	Repayment	300.00		250.00	50.00				
Mth 5	Repayment	300.00		250.00	50.00				
Mth 6	Repayment	300.00		250.00	50.00				
Mth 7	Repayment	300.00		250.00	50.00				
Mth 8	Repayment	300.00		250.00	50.00				
Mth 9	Repayment	300.00		250.00	50.00				
Mth 10	Repayment	300.00		250.00	50.00				
Mth 11	Repayment	300.00		250.00	50.00				
Mth 12	Repayment	300.00		250.00	50.00				
TOTAL		6,600.00	3,000.00	3,000.00	600.00			3,000.00	3,000.00

Figure 5.1 *Grace Morris – purchase of freezer.*

Capital allowance calculations

The rules for calculating capital allowances can vary from year to year, with the Chancellor of the Exchequer changing the percentages and details of special allowances that might apply for the next year in an annual budget statement. The examples below use a 20% rate.

At the end of the year the total of the 'Purchase of equipment' column gives the capital cost of all equipment acquired in the year, even if some of it may not have been paid for in full. There are special rules for what capital allowances can be claimed in years you buy equipment for use in your business. Currently you can usually spend up to £50,000 on business equipment and get 100% of this as a capital allowance in the year you purchase them. This is called the Annual Investment Allowance (or AIA). This allowance is likely to cover much, if not all, of your capital purchases in a year *as a small business*.

In the second or subsequent years of a business, anything of your equipment purchase cost still left without an allowance being received for it in the first year is added to the balance of what is called in the accountancy jargon the pool of 'unrelieved expenditure' from earlier years, see below. Subtract from this new pool total any amount received in the year from the sale of equipment. Finally calculate 20% of the remaining balance to give the 'writing down allowance', which is the total capital allowance available to claim that year against tax for the purchase of plant and equipment. This figure is entered onto the tax return. The remaining balance now becomes the pool of unrelieved expenditure to be carried forward into the following year's calculation.

6

petty cash

It is quite normal in a business to use cash occasionally to buy things rather than having to write cheques or use the business credit card. This is particularly true for small transactions. This chapter shows you how to do this without complicating your record keeping.

The book-keeping system outlined in this book starts from bank statements. Inevitably, however, you will pay some expenses in cash, such as items of stationery, taxi fares and so on. There are two ways to ensure that these items are correctly recorded, both based on the idea that you accumulate the cash receipts and from time to time write a cheque to cover the accumulated cost. That cheque is then treated in the same way as one paying off any other bill by simply analysing the total payment across the relevant expenditure categories.

Cheque reimbursement

The simplest approach is not to keep any sort of physical petty cash 'float' at all. When you need to pay cash you use your own money, but you must still keep the receipts carefully. Then, at (say) monthly intervals, sort those receipts into the categories of expenditure used in the cashbook. Probably most will be general administrative expenses and travel expenses. Use a separate sheet of paper and list the receipts under each category before adding up the amounts to get to separate subtotals. Add the subtotals to get the total for which the cheque is made out. Post the subtotals into the cashbook against the overall cheque total, and pay the cheque into your personal bank account.

Example

Ben Martin has receipts for a map, some de-icer, accommodation following a long trip when he could not get back that night, a pen and a book of stamps. Figure 6.1 shows how he wrote these up on a sheet of paper, and Figure 6.2 shows how he entered them into his cashbook. He paid the cheque into his own personal bank account.

Imprest petty cash system

The second method is to keep a petty cash tin, and to keep a certain cash float in it, say £100. Whenever you have paid for something in cash, put the receipt into the box and take out the amount of cash spent. If you do not have the receipt then write out

```
Motor Expenses:
7/5        De-icer                           3.49
1/6        Mapbook                           4.99
                                             8.48

    Administration Expenses
28/6       Pen                               1.19
28/6       Stamps                            2.60
                                             3.79

    Travel Expenses
2/5        Clearview B + B, Hastings        23.00


Total                                       35.27


Ch. no.  362   10.7
```

Figure 6.1 *Ben Martin's petty cash list.*

Date	Payments out	Cheque no.	Total	Cost of sales	Motor exes.	Admin	Travel
10.7	Petty cash	362	35.27		8.48	3.79	23.00

Figure 6.2 *Ben Martin's cashbook record of petty cash.*

a slip which explains what the payment is for. Printed petty cash slips are sold at stationers, although there is no reason why you cannot just use scrap paper for this. When the amount of cash in the tin gets low, cash a cheque or withdraw cash on your debit card to top up the petty cash back to the original balance of £100.

This method for petty cash is common and is known as the imprest system. Imprest is simply an archaic word meaning a loan.

7

receipts

So far this book has concentrated on how you record what you spend (your expenses) in running our business. This chapter shows you how to record details of money you receive from selling your goods or your services. Clearly this is important as without these receipts your business will not make any profits! This chapter includes a discussion of the implications of doing only cash business or providing your customers with credit. It is critical that you manage this decision carefully to make sure you are able to sustain the flow of money into your business.

In this chapter we look at receipts, which in general terms are easier to record.

We also look at the entries made in the bank paying-in book, and explain how the cashbook should be completed.

Cash or credit?

Unlike the system for the filing of purchase invoices received, there are two different situations to consider when looking at receipts. The business may be one that is run primarily on credit, where sales invoices are raised but only paid by customers later. Alternatively, the business may be one where goods or services are usually paid for at the time of sale. Even if some of these receipts are in the form of customer cheques or by credit card, this is commonly referred to as a cash business. The recording considerations vary for each of these types of business.

In a credit-based business there are generally fewer (but larger) transactions. Hardip Singh might have 50 customers in a year, whereas Grace Morris might have that many in a day. Hardip's invoices are generally paid by client cheque, so that each individual payment can be entered onto a paying-in slip, and can be related back to the sales invoice. In a cash-based business, even if a few payments are made by cheque, it is unlikely that it will be viable or sensible to try and identify individual sales transactions separately. The usual approach is to use set points at which takings are totalled, generally each day at the close of business.

Credit-based business

The standard sales filing system needed by a credit-based business is similar to that used for purchases. A sales invoice will be raised for each job completed, possibly using a pre-numbered duplicate invoice book, as sold by stationers. Using a sheet of carbon paper, as each invoice is written out a duplicate copy is left in the book. Invoices can also be produced on a computer, of course, perhaps using a word processor template.

The two essentials for an invoicing system are that the invoices should be sequentially numbered and that a duplicate copy is kept. The numbering system helps to ensure that no invoice is lost, and to reassure HM Revenue & Customs that the likelihood of error or fraud is low. Duplicate copies also provide a system for chasing unpaid bills.

Credit management

In addition to providing a record of business sales, invoices have an essential role to play in credit management. When looking at monies owed to you, you must encourage your customers to pay up promptly, and that includes following up debts more with increasing vigour as they get older.

Invoices should state the time when they are due for payment, within seven days, two weeks or a month, rarely longer. You can issue a statement (i.e. summary of invoice(s) outstanding) before that time has expired, of course.

While experience varies from business to business, most invoices get paid within 30 to 60 days of issue. An invoice outstanding for more than 90 days without good reason is often a trigger for enforcement action: either by instructing solicitors or a debt collection agency, or by personally taking out a court summons. This is neither expensive nor difficult, and a letter saying that such a summons will be issued without further warning if payment is not received in seven days may itself be a sufficient trigger to make the customer pay by return.

Debt chasing procedures require careful review of each situation, and a fine blend of tact and firmness when required. Make notes on the invoice duplicates to record what you have done to try to obtain payment, and when. Use this information to determine future credit arrangements for this customer – if you do repeated business with them – to ensure you aren't constantly chasing them for overdue debts.

Cash businesses

Never take cash from the till without leaving a note that this has been done, so that it can either be repaid later or accounted for. This is one of the most common reasons for cash businesses under-declaring profits, either deliberately or by accident, and questions in this area will often be raised during a tax investigation.

Using an electronic till will provide printed sales totals each day for the cash, cheques and credit card receipts that should be in the till, and this could be an ideal solution for Grace Morris. A useful method of cash control and record-keeping is to file these till records stapled to a sheet of A4 paper, then write on the same sheet a cash reconciliation of what was in the till, split into the different types of notes and coins, cheques and credit card receipts. Deduct any cash float that the till started with. This reconciliation should balance, or identify any 'unders' or 'overs'. If discrepancies are infrequent and small, and vary both under and over, you should have no problem with HM Revenue & Customs.

Ben Martin does not use a till because of the nature of his business, but uses a cash bag instead. He makes a point of not taking out any cash until he has totalled his takings at the end of each day. He then records takings in a cashbook which he keeps in the bag. He takes out his drawings, as explained in Chapter 2, and puts the rest of the cash to one side in a separate container, ready to be banked the following morning.

The key aim when filling in the bank paying-in book is to link the supporting information on the sales file with the bank statements and the cashbook. This should be in sufficient detail that if any one of them were lost it would be possible to recreate the records from the other.

There are differences in how the paying-in book is filled in, depending on whether the business is a credit business or a cash business.

Credit business

The aim is to reference the paying-in slip back to the invoices, so that it is possible to check that the receipts for all the sales invoices have gone into the bank account.

Example

Refer back to the receipts of Hardip Singh in the example in Chapter 2, Figure 2.3. He made two deposits during the month: on 10 June he paid in a cheque for £396.75, and on 20 June he paid in three cheques that totalled £2,750.

Mr Singh must remember to record the invoice numbers, which means that in practice the paying-in slip should be filled in before the visit to the bank, since otherwise he will not have the necessary information to hand. If he cannot do this, he should at least fill in the amounts of the individual cheques being banked on the back of the counterfoil, so sales invoice numbers can be added when he is next in his office. Other information would be available from the bank statement or the cashbook but picking up the invoice numbers themselves is a lot more difficult, particularly when several cheques are banked using a single paying-in slip.

Cash business

For a cash business, the important thing is to match up the paying-in counterfoil (stub) to the record of takings. This should not be a problem if takings are banked daily; but if more than one day's takings are banked together then it is a good idea to prepare a reconciliation on the face of the last relevant takings sheet.

You should be aware that from a tax perspective, the more checkable evidence that can be provided to support the accounting records, the better. Fill in the counterfoils with the separate amounts for each type of note and coin, corresponding to the analysis that you have on the daily takings sheet. This in itself might not have prevented a person from taking cash out of a till before 'cashing up', but it all helps to show a well-controlled process.

Cashbook headings

Using the 32-column analysis book recommended earlier, now begin the receipts analysis at column 22. Head this up as 'Date'. Above the next three columns, 23–25, write the heading 'Payments in' – you will treat these as a single column, using it to record narrative explaining what the payment was for. The narrative will often simply be 'Cash/cheques'.

The next column, 26, should be headed as 'Reference', using it for the reference number on the paying-in slip, if there is one. The next column should be headed 'Total', but leave the following column, 28, blank. It will be used for the same purpose as the column left blank on the payments side. Column 29 should be headed as 'Income', and column 30 as 'Capital introduced'.

Using the receipts columns

With the possible exception of the 'Capital introduced' column, it may by now be fairly obvious how the various columns are used.

Example

Figure 7.1 shows the entries made by Hardip Singh, completing the cashbook for the information provided in Chapter 2, Figure 2.3.

Notes

1 The same basic rule for completing the receipts analysis applies as that for payments. The total is written in the 'Total' column, and the entries in the analysis columns for each line must together add up to that amount. In practice, unless VAT is involved, the analysis will almost invariably be under the 'Income' column.

2 You may wish to analyse sales income over more than one column for your own information. If, for example, there are two or more distinct sides to your business, and you can easily distinguish between receipts for each, then it may be worth recording extra information to help with calculations of which are making the most profit. Grace Morris, for

| Date | Payments in | | | Ref. | Total | | Income | Cap. Int. |
22	23	24	25	26	27	28	29	30
10.6	Cheques			132	396.75			396.75
20.6	Cheques			133	2750.00			2750.00

Figure 7.1 *Hardip Singh's cashbook – receipts side.*

example, might want to set up the shop's electronic till by using different sales 'codes' to record the various stock lines that she sells, separating newspapers and magazines from food sales, for example. To make fullest use of this information it would also be necessary to split the recording for cost of sales as well, to enable each category of sales to be set against the cost of sales for that category, and to thus produce what accountants would call the 'gross profit' for each.

8

capital introduced

When you start your business you will need to put in money (your own probably, in part at least) to get started. You might also give equipment to the business. Once the business is functioning you might need to put in more of your own money from time to time to keep it going. This all needs to be carefully recorded so that you are sure of the total amount the business owes you. In this chapter we show you how to do this in our simple system.

Capital introduced into a business is the opposite of drawings. Whereas drawings are sums taken out of a business by its proprietor, capital introduced represents monies belonging to the proprietor that have been put into the business.

Simple introduction of capital

The most straightforward introduction of capital to a business is when a lump sum is paid into the business bank account. In that situation, the narrative describes where the money came from, and the analysis goes under 'Capital introduced'.

Example

Hardip Singh sold some shares for £5,000, and paid the proceeds into the business account in order to reduce the overdraft. Figure 8.1 shows how the entry is recorded.

Date 22	Payments in 23	24	25	Ref. 26	Total 27	28	Income 29	Cap. Int. 30
7.8	Cheque (BT shares)			154	5000			5000

Figure 8.1 *Hardip Singh – capital introduced.*

Note

It is important to record a clear explanation of where any capital introduced came from. The risk is that at a later stage HM Revenue & Customs may try to suggest that it came from business takings that had not been declared and which had been kept hidden.

More complex transactions

Two transactions that needed to be accounted for as capital introduced arose in earlier chapters: the purchase of equipment on credit and the part payment of a credit card bill. Refer back to Chapter 5 to refresh your memory. All funds coming into the business which are not business income are treated in this system as capital introduced. Set out below are some other examples.

Loans

In this system, any injection of funds into a business must be recorded as capital introduced, and any repayments recorded as drawings. The payment of the interest charges will be an expense.

Example 1

The facts in Figure 8.2 are the same as those in Figure 8.1 above, except that the £5,000 injected into the bank account this time came from a loan taken out by Mr Singh in order to consolidate his overdraft. He has to repay the new loan at £200 each month, of which he calculates that £150 is capital repayment of the loan itself and £50 is interest charges.

The opposite of drawings is capital introduced. So far all repayments of the loan have been treated as drawings, as if they were repayments of capital. In fact, £200 of the total repayment comprised interest charges. Therefore drawings need to be reduced by £200, and the easiest way to do that is to increase capital introduced by £200.

Date	Payments out	Ref.	Total	Interest	Drawings
7.9	Transfer (loan rept.)		200.00	50.00	150.00

Date	Payments in	Ref.	Total	Cap. Int.	
7.8	Transfer (loan)		5000.00	5000.00	

Figure 8.2 *Hardip Singh – loan and repayment.*

Equipment introduced

This area is much more straightforward, and again requires contra entries. On occasion the business owner may put assets directly into the business rather than cash. In that case each asset needs to be placed under the heading of purchase of equipment, but because the balance at the bank will not itself have changed, a contra entry will be needed. Since the overall position is exactly the same as if funds to buy the asset had been put into the business by the proprietor, and the asset then purchased from a third party, the transaction is recorded as if that had in fact happened. The owner will need to place a fair open-market value on the asset at the time of its introduction to the business.

Example

Figure 8.3 shows the situation after Grace Morris had inherited an estate car worth £8,000. The amount to be entered for the transaction is £8,000; for tax purposes the asset must be shown at its market value at the time it was taken into the business. The introduction of the car is shown on the payments side of her cashbook as a contra item under 'Equipment purchased'. Note in passing that tax allowances (capital allowances) will be available on the car as explained in Chapter 5, even though Mrs Morris did not actually pay anything for it. On the receipts side of the cashbook the contra entry goes under 'Capital introduced'.

Date	Payments out	Ref.	Total	Equipment
1.9	Contra (car inherited)		8,000.00	8,000.00

Date	Payments in	Ref.	Total	Cap. Int.
1.9	Contra (car inherited)		8,000.00	8,000.00

Figure 8.3 *Grace Morris – equipment introduced.*

Items not treated as capital introduced

There are some entries that can be misleading. An example is if a direct debit against the account 'bounces' (is not paid because there are not enough funds in the account). This will be shown on the bank statement in the way set out in Figure 8.4. The debit to BT for £450 appears to have gone through when it was called for by BT's bank, but this made the account overdrawn. As there was no overdraft facility in place, the debit was not actually paid, and was subsequently credited back onto the bank statement.

		Debit	Credit	Balance
3.7	DD BT	450.00		−125.67
3.7	Unpaid direct debit		450.00	324.33

Figure 8.4 *Unpaid direct debit.*

The simplest treatment is to put a line through both entries on the bank statement and not record it at all; when you think about it, the transaction did not ever actually happen.

end of
month
procedures
and VAT

Each month you should compare your cashbook with your bank statement as you receive it to check you agree with the bank what cash your business has at that stage. This is important for a number of reasons: you might have forgotten to record everything in your cashbook by accident; you might have made a mistake in your recording of specific items; maybe you don't have paperwork for a transaction because it was done directly at the bank (e.g. standing orders or direct debits perhaps). Your monthly comparison (called a reconciliation) of these two documents is a critical part of keeping your records fully up to date.

This chapter concludes with a discussion of VAT and considers whether you have to register to charge this, and if so how you handle this in your accounts.

Reconciliation

After all business accounting transactions have been entered into the analysed cashbook each month, they need to be reconciled to the bank account. The cashbook page must be checked and totalled and a new page started for the next month. The type of bank reconciliation depends upon the way that records are kept. For Hardip Singh, the reconciliation is an integral part of the process of completing his books, since he doesn't write them up until the bank statement is available for the month. He then spends a couple of hours doing the book-keeping entries. Starting with the payments, he enters each transaction in turn from his bank statement into the cashbook, both in the 'Total' column and under the appropriate analysis column. He is able to get the information for the analysis from the cheque-book stub and/or the file of paid bills. During this process he places a tick on the bottom of the stub for each cheque that has cleared through the bank. After entering all the payments in this way he looks through the cheque book to identify any cheques written before the end of the month but which have not yet passed through the bank account, and he lists these on the bank statement.

Mr Singh then adds each column, and checks that the totals of all the analysis columns add up to the same figure as does the 'Total' column itself. This process is repeated for the receipts side of the cashbook.

The final entry in the cashbook each month is to subtract the total of 'Payments out' from total receipts, including the balance brought forward (whichever side it was on). The result should be the same as the balance on the bank statement; positive if in credit and negative if overdrawn. This figure becomes the balance taken forward to the next page, where the headings are written in and the balance brought forward is entered for the next month.

The final version of Mr Singh's cashbook after it has been completed for June, using the earlier entries from Figure 2.5, is shown in Figure 9.1.

Mr Singh then goes through the paying-in book to see if any deposits made have not yet been credited on the business bank

Bank account no 123 456 23   Sort code 22-22-22   June 201X

Date	Payments out	Cheque no.	Total	Cost of sales	Employees	Admin.	Motor	Travel	Advertising	Legal/Prof.	Finance	Drawings
1 Jun	Bal b/f		2,040.53	2,040.53								
3 Jun	s/o County Leasing		345.22				345.22					
8 Jun	High St Garage	234	28.34				28.34					
10 Jun	V G Browns		25.68			25.68						
12 Jun	s/o H Singh		500.00									500.00
14 Jun	Charges		42.30								42.30	
18 Jun	Anytown Courier	235	43.69						43.69			
18 Jun	Smarts	237	692.59	662.59								30.00
21 Jun	DD NICO		28.40									28.40
23 Jun	Jones Plumb.	238	254.00	254.00								
23 Jun	Post Office Limited	239	150.00				150.00					
28 Jun	Print Presto	241	82.38			82.38						
30 Jun	DD Magnificent Mutual		100.00									100.00
30 Jun	TOTALS		4333.13	916.59		108.06	523.56		43.69		42.30	658.40

Figure 9.1 *Hardip Singh – end of month.*

statement. If they were paid into the account in the few days before the end of the month they should appear on the next statement. He simply lists these missing credits on the front of the current statement.

Finally he adds any missing receipts and subtracts any missing cheque payments from the balance on the statement. This provides the true bank balance (or overdraft) at the statement date.

VAT

Although VAT will be suffered on many goods and services that a business purchases, this tax is just treated as part of the purchase price unless the business proprietor registers for VAT.

It is compulsory to register for VAT once sales of goods or services liable to VAT exceed the VAT registration limit. The latest registration threshold is available from HM Revenue & Customs. Once registered, the proprietor must charge VAT on all taxable supplies.

Accounting principles

When a business is VAT-registered, there is a key concept to bear in mind. Since the business is in effect acting as a tax collector, the VAT that it charges on sales is not the business's money at all, and thus it is important you don't treat it as your income. Instead it is kept separate until the time comes to complete the VAT return. Similarly, for a VAT-registered business the true cost of anything is the net (VAT-exclusive) cost, and this is the amount to record as an expense or as the cost of equipment. VAT suffered must be considered as something separate from costs, reclaimable in due course when the VAT return is completed.

Cashbook entries – payments

For a VAT-registered business, the way the VAT is recorded in the analysed cashbook is to add a separate column in the analysis, both for payments and for receipts. Figure 9.2 shows again the

Date	Details	Total	Motor	Admin.	Drawings	Finance	Advertising	Cost of sales	VAT
3 Jun	s/o County Leasing	345.22	287.68						57.54
8 Jun	234 High St Garage	28.34	23.62						4.72
10 Jun	V G Browns	25.68	21.40						4.28
12 Jun	s/o H Singh	500.00			500.00				
14 Jun	Charges	42.30				42.30			
18 Jun	235 Anytown Courier	43.69					36.41		7.28
18 Jun	237 Smarts	692.59			30.00			552.16	110.43
21 Jun	DD NICO	28.40			28.40				
23 Jun	238 Jones Plumb.	254.00						211.67	42.33
23 Jun	239 Post Office Limited	150.00	150.00						
28 Jun	241 Print Presto	82.38		68.65					13.73
30 Jun	DD Magnificent Mutual	100.00			100.00				
30 Jun	TOTALS	2292.60	482.70	68.65	658.40	42.30	36.41	763.83	240.31

Figure 9.2 *Hardip Singh – analysed payments for June, if VAT-registered.*

analysed payments for June for Hardip Singh, but this time on the basis that he is VAT-registered. Expenses with VAT on them have been further analysed, with VAT-exclusive amounts shown under the appropriate analysis columns and the VAT itself written in a separate column at the end. Sometimes the VAT column is placed after the 'Total' column.

Notes

1 Equipment leasing costs are generally subject to VAT.

2 The van is used for business purposes and so VAT on fuel can be reclaimed, provided that Mr Singh remembers to obtain a VAT invoice from the garage as evidence. A VAT invoice must show the supplier's VAT registration number.

3 For costs over £30 a proper VAT invoice should be requested from suppliers. The amount of VAT (at 20%) can always be calculated by multiplying the VAT-inclusive price by 1/6.

4 Bank charges and interest are VAT-exempt items, as are vehicle road fund licences.

5 Care must be taken in dealing with the entry for the purchases from Smarts. The total purchases came to £692.59, but £30 of this was for private use and VAT can only be claimed back on business purchases. The £30 in drawings does not change, and 1/6 of the amount previously under 'Cost of sales' is shown as the input VAT of £110.43 reclaimable only on the business items.

6 The 'VAT' column is treated like any other in the analysis; it is totalled and brought into the cross-check calculation to ensure that the total of the analysis columns equals the total of the 'Total' column. Totals under the other analysis columns have reduced to match the amount now shown under the 'VAT' column.

Cashbook entries – receipts

Figure 9.3 shows the receipts side of Mr Singh's cashbook for June. The VAT fraction, 1/6, of receipts is now treated as VAT. Although the costs of the purchases made have been reduced

| Date | Payments in | | Ref. | Total | | Income | Cap Int. | VAT |
22	23	24	25	26	27	28	29	30	
10.6	Cheques		132		396.75		330.62		66.13
20.6	Cheques		133		2750.00		2291.66		458.34
					3146.75		2622.28		524.47

Figure 9.3 *Hardip Singh – analysed receipts for June if VAT-registered.*

slightly by the ability of the business to reclaim VAT, this cost reduction is more than outweighed by the reduction in value of sales that now suffer VAT.

End of quarter

At regular intervals (usually quarterly) a VAT return must be made. Provided you are able to report on a cash basis, which is the normal basis for smaller businesses (seek advice if you are unsure), you simply add up the VAT totals recorded in your cashbook for the period. This gives the total VAT on outputs (sales) for the period, and the total VAT on inputs (costs).

When the VAT cheque is written in the cashbook, it can be included under the 'VAT' column for payments. As a result, if there were no further entries between the time when the quarter ended and when the VAT cheque was paid over, the total in the payments 'VAT' column would now match the total in the receipts 'VAT' column. In practice, because a month is allowed for completing the return and making the payment, the normal position will be a balance permanently in favour of the 'Receipts' column. This balance will increase as the end of the VAT period approaches, then drops back to a low figure when the cheque is paid out to HM Revenue & Customs.

10
end of year totals

Once a year you will be required to summarize the activities of your business. All businesses are required to do this so the details are available for tax purposes, but it is also useful to review annually (at least) how the business has gone compared to what you were expecting, and to use this information to set your plans for the next year. This chapter shows you what you need to do to prepare your cashbook to produce these summaries.

The information given in the previous chapters is all that is needed to keep your accounting records on a day-to-day basis. If you intend to use an accountant to complete the figures and prepare your income tax return you need only complete the calculations in this chapter, then hand the records over to the accountant. If, however, you decide to handle your own financial affairs, this chapter and those that follow demonstrate two different methods for producing your end of year results.

The first approach is designed to produce the income and expenditure information needed to complete a tax return. For a smaller business, where the owner knows the financial position of the business and requires no extra financial information, then nothing else will be required. There is no legal requirement for a small sole trader business to produce full accounts.

However, some businesses may need to produce a full set of financial statements, with a profit and loss account and a 'balance sheet', the latter showing the assets and the liabilities of the business. These may be required by the bank, for example, or by a potential purchaser. They can also provide useful information to a business owner who understands how to interpret them. We will look at the process in the next chapter.

The case study that will be used for the first approach is Ben Martin: his is typically the sort of business that may not need any more detail about its financial performance than the profit figure on which income tax is due.

Cashbook totals

After ruling off and totalling the figures for the last month of the business year, March in this case, the final year end totals must be produced. The next page in the cashbook should be headed up as 'Year ended 31 March 201X – Summary'. Enter the usual headings at the top of the analysis columns.

In the wide column in which the details of cheque payments are normally entered, write the months of the trading year, one on each line. Starting with April, copy the totals from each month's cashbook page onto this summary, so each line summarizes the totals for that month. Remember to include the blank columns to the right of the totals for both payments and receipts, which you used in the analysis to bring forward the balances from the previous month.

Next add up each of the columns again, in order to get to the annual totals. In exactly the same way as the monthly totals, the analysis columns for payments must add up to the same figure as the 'Payments total' column, and the analysis columns for the receipts must add up to the same as its 'Total' column.

Example

Figure 10.1 shows the year end summary for Ben Martin, on the payments side of the analysis book. Columns which he did not use have been omitted.

He was always in credit with the bank, and so there are no entries in the blank column to the right of the total. The figure at the bottom of the 'Total' column shows that payments made in the year totalled £17,278.56, and the analysis columns that follow show what the money was spent on. A total of £8,952.18 was, in fact, not spent on business items at all, it was his drawings figure for the year.

Adjustment for balances brought forward

You may well find that the figure showing in one or both totals columns looks rather high. The reason for this is that the totals include the balances brought forward each month on the business bank account. If during the year the business fluctuated between a credit bank balance and an overdraft, both payments and receipts totals will be overstated.

Eliminate all of these monthly brought forward balances. Whatever figure appears in either (or both) of the columns totalling the brought forward balances, write it in the same column on the line underneath, but in brackets, and also write it underneath the 'Total' column in brackets. Then subtract it from the figure above. When you subtract this figure from itself there will be nothing

Month	Total	Cost of sales	Admin.	Motor	Travel/ Subs.	Advertising	Drawings
April	1,297.26	143.80	23.46	350.00		140.00	640.00
May	1,202.79	213.45		430.34	34.00		525.00
June	1,138.54	123.54	12.00	350.00			653.00
July	2,177.01	134.29	45.23	654.23		54.00	1,289.26
August	1,190.89	210.89		385.00			595.00
September	1,191.53	145.29	16.24	350.00			680.00
October	1,744.41	134.93		723.94		265.54	620.00
November	1,367.26	218.82		382.23	68.21		698.00
December	1,374.81	268.23	22.58	350.00			734.00
January	2,138.32	187.20		480.00	25.20	120.00	1,325.92
February	1,321.46	162.00	76.23	541.23			542.00
March	1,134.28	134.28		350.00			650.00
Total	17,278.56	2,076.72	195.74	5,346.97	127.41	579.54	8,952.18

Figure 10.1 *Ben Martin's payments year end summary.*

left in the 'Brought forward' column. The 'Total' column will also be reduced by the same amount. As a result the figures will still balance. Add the figures in the analysis columns, and now that there is nothing in the 'Brought forward' column the total must be equal to the new figure in the 'Total' column.

Example

This can be seen in Figure 10.2, showing the receipts side of the year end summary for Ben Martin. The 'Total' column adds up to £53,513.74, but this figure is meaningless. All of the brought

	Total	Brought fwd.	Income	Cap.Int.
April	4,060.90	2,496.92	1,563.98	
May	4,312.87	2,763.64	1,349.23	200.00
June	4,239.20	2,710.08	1,529.12	
July	4,587.89	3,100.66	1,487.23	
August	3,564.00	2,410.88	1,029.12	124.00
September	4,118.26	2,373.11	1,745.15	
October	4,551.97	2,926.73	1,625.24	
November	4,304.85	2,807.56	1,497.29	
December	4,987.71	2,937.59	2,025.12	25.00
January	5,306.19	3,612.90	1,693.29	
February	4,636.12	3,167.87	1,468.25	
March	4,843.78	3,314.66	1,529.12	
Total	53,513.74	34,622.60	18,542.14	349.00
	(34,622.60)	(34,622.60)		
	18,891.14			

Figure 10.2 Ben Martin's receipts year end summary.

forward bank balances (of about £3,000 each month) have been included within it. These add up to £34,622.60. This figure must be eliminated from the total to arrive at the true amount that has been paid into the account, namely £18,891.14.

General principles

The totals figures derived above showed how much money was spent during the year and how much money was received. The difference between the two is not necessarily the profit (or loss) for the year.

For example, suppose Mr Dylan bought 100 CDs for £5 each. He sold them all during the month for £10 each. His income and expenditure figures show purchases totalling £500 and sales of £1,000. Now suppose Mr John purchased 200 CDs for £5 each. He sold 100 of them during the month for £10 each. His income and expenditure figures show purchases of £1,000 and sales of £1,000.

Would it be correct to say Mr Dylan made £500 profit in the month whereas Mr John merely broke even? Mr John sold as many CDs as Mr Dylan, and made the same amount of profit on each one. The difference is that Mr John still had some left over to sell in the future. He had some 'closing stock' remaining at the end of the month.

A similar problem can arise for bills received but not yet accounted for. For example, Mr John might have been invoiced for his 200 CDs but not yet paid the bill. If he sold 100 of them his books would show receipts totalling £1,000 but no payments. It would be wrong to state that he had made £1,000 profit simply because he had not paid for the CDs which he had sold.

Adjusting for these timing differences is necessary to move from a simplistic cash receipts and payments basis to what is known as the earnings (or what accountants call the 'accruals') basis.

Cost of sales

To reach an accurate cost of sales figure, a physical count of stock is needed to determine how much stock remains unsold at the end of the year. This closing stock can then be valued at its original cost, or, if it has fallen in value since it was purchased, at the value that it could now be sold for. This means that stock will be valued at cost unless it could now be sold only at a loss.

A manufacturing business could have three different types of stock: raw materials, uncompleted manufacturing work in progress and finally the finished goods themselves. Each type must be valued. For raw materials the principles are straightforward, but when valuing work in progress and finished goods at 'cost' an allowance must be made not just for the raw materials used, but also for the wages, heat, light, etc. that have gone into the manufacturing process.

Service businesses do not have stock, but may have carried out work which has not yet been billed to the customer. This is also accounted for as work in progress. We will review how to deal with this in the next chapter.

Other adjustments

The other year end adjustments needed are generally easier to calculate. At the end of the year write 'unpaid at year end' on the face of each invoice in the filing system that is still above the divider card as not yet paid. Then list these unpaid bills and total them up under each respective category of expenditure. Include the VAT-exclusive figure only if you are VAT-registered, since the VAT element will be reclaimable anyway in due course. If you are not VAT-registered, include the full amount.

Recording the adjustments

The stock valuation and the expense category totals for the unpaid bills now need to be entered under the payments side of the year end summary, a couple of lines below the totals, and any adjustments made following guidance in the last chapter. In the details column write 'Stock at year end' and write the total figure for stock under the 'Cost of sales' column. Put brackets round it, as it is to be deducted in order to reduce the cost of sales in the year by the value of stock remaining unsold at the year end.

If this is not the first year of trading then the closing stock figure from the end of the previous year must now be added to this year's cost of sales figure. On the next line of the summary write 'Stock at beginning of the year' and write it in under 'Cost of sales'. The total under the 'Cost of sales' column will now show the true 'Cost of sales' for the year.

A similar process is needed to deal with the unpaid purchase invoices. On the next line, write 'Creditors at year end'. Creditors are suppliers who are owed money by the business. Calculate the totals under the appropriate headings. These are added to the totals already paid in the year, because they are costs that have been incurred in the year even though the invoices themselves have not yet been paid. On the next line (again, unless this is the first set of accounts for the business where you won't have any), write 'Creditors at start of year' and fill in the figures from the previous year end, using brackets as they are to be deducted. Complete the totals to arrive at the true costs under each heading on a full accruals basis.

Debtors

Debtors are customers who owe monies to the business. To calculate the year end figure, write 'unpaid at year end' on all invoices issued but not yet paid on 31 March (or whatever your year end is if it not this date). Enter them on the year end summary in the same way as the adjustment for creditors in the last chapter. Add the debtors at the end of the current year, and subtract (i.e. remove from total receipts in the year) any debtors that were outstanding at the end of the previous year.

Businesses that sell on credit risk suffering bad debts, where it proves impossible to recover money owed to the business. If this occurs with one of your debts simply draw a line through the sales invoice and ignore it, do not include it in the debtors total at all. Since the debt will not have been included on the receipts side of the analysed cashbook, it is treated as if it had never arisen in the first place.

However, if some uncertainty exists about whether a bill will be paid, it is possible to make what is called a 'provision for doubtful debts'. HM Revenue & Customs will only allow a tax deduction for doubtful debts if they are 'specific', that is related to a particular bill. For tax purposes you are not permitted to say that, on average, you find 5% of your debts go bad and you are therefore going to make a 5% provision against all monies owed to the business at the year end. For a bad debt provision to be tax allowable you have to be able to say that you expect a particular debt to go bad for a specific reason and make a specific provision against that debt.

Work in progress

The other adjustment that may be needed is for work in progress. The difficulty for service-based businesses is typically that clients are billed only when work is complete, whereas at the year end some work will still be in progress. However, if some of the costs of carrying out the work have been incurred, it is correct that this work in progress should be valued at cost and added to the sales for the year.

From a practical point of view, if the business consists of providing only the proprietor's own skills and labour, with no other direct costs for particular jobs nor costs of employing staff to do any of the work, the adjustment for unfinished work in progress is ignored. The proprietor's own time and effort is not treated as a cost to the business for this purpose.

If you are in any doubt about the need to make a work in progress adjustment, ask for advice from a qualified accountant or from HM Revenue & Customs.

The entry is made in the normal way: simply add the value of work in progress at the end of the current year to receipts, and subtract any work in progress at the end of the previous year.

11

trial balance and final accounts

In this chapter we explore how to create your final accounts for the year from your cashbook record summaries. The initial step for this process is to create a trial balance to check all the entries in your cashbook are complete. You may then have some further annual adjustments to make to your records before you create your profit and loss statement and your balance sheet as the final summary records of your year.

This chapter deals with more detailed accounting, and will allow the preparation of a set of accounts in a standard 'profit and loss account' plus 'balance sheet' format. It is not possible in this book to show more than the basic mechanics of producing accounts.

The firm recommendation here is to avoid putting together a full set of accounts unless you absolutely have to. In practice, the figures entered into your tax return including those for capital allowances, as explained in the previous chapters, together with an analysis of the debtors, creditors, stock and bank balances, may well be sufficient financial management information for most smaller businesses so you won't need to produce these statements unless you want to, or someone asks you to.

Profit and loss versus balance sheet

A profit and loss account and a balance sheet each provide different information about the activities and financial position of a business. A profit and loss account summarizes the revenues and costs of a business over a stated period, often a year. A balance sheet shows the assets of a business, and its liabilities, at close of play on the last day of that period.

A balance sheet is called a balance sheet because it balances! It shows all assets owned by the business (vehicles, equipment, stock, debtors and any money at the bank), less any monies owed by the business (its liabilities). The liabilities of a business include amounts owed back to the owner(s) which accountants call owner's equity or capital.

Using what is called the double-entry accounting system (as we mentioned in the Introduction this is a more detailed alternative accounting system that many businesses use as their activities get more complicated) there are two entries for everything: a debit entry and a credit entry. Up to this point, the system in this book has not referred to debits and credits, although all entries made in the cashbook have been entered twice, once in the 'Total' column and once in the appropriate analysis column, so there is a form of double entry being used, just not in a formal way. On the payments side of the cashbook, the entries in the 'Total' column are in effect the credit entries to the bank account, and the entries in the analysis columns are the corresponding debit entries, representing costs being paid, drawings taken, or assets acquired.

On the receipts side of the cashbook, entries in the 'Total' column are in effect the debit entries to the bank account, monies received, and the entries in the analysis columns the corresponding credit entries, items of income or capital introduced to the business.

For a VAT-registered business, the entries on the payments side are debit entries showing VAT reclaimable from HM Revenue & Customs; the entries on the receipts side are credit entries showing VAT amounts due to HM Revenue & Customs.

Trial balance

This explanation is needed so you can understand how a trial balance is created, and what it illustrates for us in an accounting system. A trial balance is simply a listing of all debit and credit totals shown in the accounting records. After making all the adjustments shown in Chapter 10, what we are now referring to as debits and credits will balance (if all your entries are correct). 'Total payments out' is a credit figure, matched by the total debits shown by the analysis columns for payments. The total payments in/receipts figure is a debit, matched by the total of the analysis columns for receipts, which are all credit entries.

To draw up a trial balance, first convert the figures produced in Chapter 10 into a vertical format. Start on a new page of the cashbook, and write the headings down the wide column on the left-hand side. The first heading will be 'Bank', the others will reflect the column headings used in your cashbook. Only one VAT heading is needed, however (see Figure 11.1).

Next write across the first two cash columns the word 'Cashbook', and label the first column 'Dr' (for 'debit') and label the second one 'Cr' (for 'credit'). Begin by entering the total payments figure into the 'Cr' column and the total receipts figure into the

'Dr' column, both against a heading 'Bank'. Then enter each of the analysis totals for payments made into the 'Dr' column opposite the appropriate heading, and enter the receipts analysis totals against the appropriate headings in the 'Cr' column. The only two headings which will have an entry in both 'Dr' and 'Cr' columns are 'Bank' and 'VAT' (if VAT-registered). Now add up the 'Dr' and the 'Cr' columns and check that they still balance!

Unless this is your first year of trading, head up the next two columns as 'Opening balance' and label them 'Dr' and 'Cr' again. This is where you have to enter the final balances from the previous year end balance sheet. If you don't have a balance sheet from the previous year, but this is not your first year of trading, you would need to draw one up. That is beyond the scope of this book and is perhaps a job for an accountant to help with.

By looking carefully at the previous balance sheet, it should be quite easy to see which balances are debits and which are credits, and how they balance when set off against each other. The debit balances are the assets: equipment, stock, debtors and bank/cash. These are most of the entries at the top of the balance sheet. The credit balances are the liabilities, amounts owed to suppliers ('creditors') and any overdraft amount owed to the bank. The main credit balance after those is likely to be right at the bottom of the balance sheet, being the figure of profit retained in the business and 'owed' by the business back to the proprietor.

Add new headings in the trial balance wide left-hand column for all of these items, except for 'Equipment' and 'Bank' which have been set up as trial balance headings already. Then enter the debit and credit balances from the previous balance sheet into the 'Opening balance' columns. Add up the two columns and check they still match.

The opening balances and the cashbook movements for the year have now been entered. To end this chapter, Figure 11.1 shows Grace Morris's trial balance; the figures used have been rounded to make things easier to follow. Next we will show you how to make other necessary adjustments in order to produce final accounts.

	Cashbook		Opening balance	
	Dr	Cr	Dr	Cr
Bank	93,000	85,500	6,000	
Cost of sales (purchases)	50,000			
Employee costs	4,000			
Premises costs	5,000			
Administrative	1,000			
Motor	1,000			
Advertising	500			
Finance charges	1,500			
Equipment	2,500		4,000	
Drawings	15,000			
Income (sales)		85,000		
Capital introduced		1,000		
VAT	5,000	7,000		
Stock			3,000	
Debtors			500	
Cash			100	
Creditors				1,000
Profit retained				12,600
Depreciation				
Profit for year				
	178,500	178,500	3,600	13,600

Figure 11.1 *Opening balances and cashbook movements.*

Adjusting payments

At this point please refer back to Chapter 10. The adjustments that you are about to make are the same as those that were described there.

The only adjustments to creditors shown here are for cost of sales. If there are other creditors at the year end then other expense headings will need to be adjusted similarly.

Label the next two cash columns as 'Payments' and then mark them 'Dr' and 'Cr' respectively. The first step is the equivalent of 'adding back' the opening stock and the opening creditors to purchases.

Make a 'Cr' entry against the stock figure to remove the 'Dr' opening stock balance, and then make a matching 'Dr' entry against the purchases figure to ensure that the total cost of sales figure for the year also includes all stock already owned on the first day of the year. Next make a 'Dr' entry against the creditors opening balance figure to remove it, and then make a matching 'Cr' entry against the purchases line so that the purchases figure for the year correctly shows the impact of the brought forward creditor for purchases.

Now in the 'Dr' column enter the closing balance for stock at the year end, and in the 'Cr' column enter the year end closing balance figure for creditors. Make matching and opposite entries against the purchases line, so that the year's purchases figure correctly reflects both year end stock levels and also the creditors for purchases that exist at the year end but which have not yet been paid.

Add the two columns up, and check that they balance.

A similar exercise must now be carried out for receipts. Label the next two cash columns as 'Receipts' and enter 'Dr' and 'Cr' respectively. Enter the opening balance for debtors against the heading in the 'Cr' column, and make a corresponding entry in the 'Dr' column against the sales line. Enter the year end closing balance for debtors against the same heading, but in the 'Dr' column, and enter the same amount in the 'Cr' column on the sales line. Total the two columns to confirm that the entries match because the columns balance.

Figure 11.2 shows Grace Morris's entries for the 'Debtors' and 'Creditors' columns – the other headings are omitted for simplicity. She had the following to adjust for:

* Creditors were £2,000 at year end but only £1,000 at the start of the year.

	Payments		Receipts		Other adj.	
	Dr	Cr	Dr	Cr	Dr	Cr
Bank						
Cost of sales (purchases)	2,000 3,000	3,500 1,000				
Employee costs						
Premises costs						
Administrative						
Motor						
Advertising						
Finance charges						
Equipment						1,300
Drawings						
Income (sales)			500	800		50
Capital introduced						
VAT						
Stock	3,500	3,000				
Debtors			800	500		
Cash					50	
Creditors	1,000	2,000				
Profit retained						
Depreciation					1,300	
Profit for year						
	9,500	9,500	1,300	1,300	1,350	1,350

Figure 11.2 *Payments, receipts and adjustments.*

* Debtors (for newspapers) totalled £800 at the year end, £500 at the start.
* Stock £3,500 at the year end, £3,000 at the start.
* Depreciation charge £1,300 for the year. Depreciation is a cost entry needed to reflect the decrease in value of long-term assets such as equipment and vehicles (see below).
* Cash on hand £50 at the year end, £100 at the start.

Other adjustments

Head up the next two cash columns as 'Other adjustments'. As explained in Chapter 10 there are a number of matters which can be reflected in the accounts, but the key one is depreciation.

Depreciation has not been mentioned so far, partly because it is not taken into account for tax purposes and capital allowances are given instead. The idea of depreciation is that a figure should be written off as an expense each year to reflect the fall in value of plant and equipment during that year. In practice many small businesses use a set formula such as 20% a year.

Enter a new heading in the left-hand column, an expense heading, called 'Depreciation expense'. Enter in the 'Dr' column of 'Other adjustments' the likely (it is almost certainly an estimate) depreciation charge for the year, and in the 'Cr' column enter the same amount against the heading for equipment cost.

Final accounts

Label the next two columns 'Profit and loss account' and the following two 'Balance sheet', using 'Dr' and 'Cr' headings as before. You are now going to total the figures across for each line, and enter the final figure in the appropriate column for either profit and loss or balance sheet. The easiest way to do this is to work on the profit and loss figures first, because these are all the headings that appeared in the analysed cashbook, but excluding bank, VAT, drawings, capital introduced and equipment purchased. There is also the new heading for the depreciation charge (i.e. expense).

All of the other headings will be totalled and the totals shown under the 'Balance sheet' columns.

Now add up each row, but look first to see whether, overall, the credits or the debits are higher. With most lines this should be quite easy because all expense lines are going to end up as debit totals, all income lines as credit totals. Assets will be debits, liabilities will be credits. For totals which are going to end up as debits, add up all the debits in that row, deduct the credits and enter the balance in the 'Dr' column of 'Profit and loss' if the item is an expense item, or put it in the 'Dr' column of 'Balance sheet' otherwise.

With totals that are going to end up as credits it is the other way round: add up the credits, deduct the debits, and put the result in the 'Cr' column. You should now find that the figures for closing stock, debtors and creditors will all be as you expect; and the year end bank balance should also be correct. If you think about the entries made this is not surprising. The system takes into account the starting bank balance, adjust for total receipts and total payments, and thus the result must (should!) be the closing balance.

The final step is to add a last new heading to the left-hand column, called 'Profit for year'. Add up the total of the 'Cr' column under 'Profit and loss', then subtract all the entries in the 'Dr' column. Enter the difference in the 'Dr' column of 'Profit and loss' and the 'Cr' column of 'Balance sheet'. If when you are doing this difference calculation you find that the total of the 'Dr' column exceeds that of the 'Cr' column then the business has made a loss, and the difference figure goes the other way around when writing it into the trial balance. Put a loss into the 'Cr' column of 'Profit and loss' and into the 'Dr' column of 'Balance sheet'.

The last stage is to enter these figures from the trial balance columns onto a set of accounts. This is really just a matter of setting out the figures into an accepted format. Follow the example in Figure 11.3 for Grace Morris. Note that if she was overdrawn at the bank, the bank figure would appear as a credit in the 'Balance sheet' columns of the trial balance, and would appear with 'Creditors' in the balance sheet itself.

Balance sheet

Fixed assets:

Equipment		5,200

Current assets:

Stock	3,500	
Debtors	800	
Bank	13,500	
Cash	150	
	17,950	

Current liabilities:

Creditors	2,000	
VAT	2,000	
Net current assets	4,000	
		13,950
		19,150

Represented by:

Profit retained	12,600	
Profit for year	20,550	
Capital introduced	1,000	
	34,150	
Less drawings	(15,000)	
		19,150

Figure 11.3a *Final accounts for Grace Morris: balance sheet.*

Profit and loss account

Sales		85,350
Less: Cost of sales		(50,500)
Gross profit		34,850
Less:		
Employee costs	4,000	
Premises costs	5,000	
Administrative	1,000	
Motor	1,000	
Advertising	500	
Finance charges	1,500	
Depreciation	1,300	
		(14,300)
Net profit for the year		20,550

Figure 11.3b *Final accounts for Grace Morris: profit and loss account.*

12

computerization